D0382241

ST. JOHN THE BAPTIST ELEMENTARY
LIBRARY MEDIA CENTER

A
16th CENTURY
MOSQUE

Series Editor	David Salariya
Book Editor	Jenny Millington
Consultant	Richard Tames

Author:
Fiona Macdonald is a graduate of Newnham College, Cambridge. She has written many books on historical subjects for children and teachers, and has contributed to television programs on medieval topics. She is a part-time tutor at the University of East Anglia.

Illustrator:
Mark Bergin was born in Hastings in 1961. He studied at Eastbourne College of Art and has specialized in historical reconstruction since leaving art school in 1983. He lives in East Sussex with his wife and daughter.

Consultant:
Richard Tames is the author of *Approaches to Islam* and *The Muslim World*. He was formerly Head of External Services at the University of London's School of Oriental and African Studies.

Acknowledgment:
The author would like to thank Mrs Farhat Din for her comments and advice.

Created, designed and produced by
The Salariya Book Co Ltd, Brighton, UK

Published by
PETER BEDRICK BOOKS
2112 Broadway
New York, NY 10023

© The Salariya Book Co Ltd MCMXCIV

All rights reserved. No part of this book may be reproduced, stored in a retrieval system, or transmitted in any form or by any means, electronic, mechanical, photocopying, recording or otherwise, without the prior permission of the copyright owner.

Published by agreement with Simon & Schuster Young Books, England

Library of Congress Cataloging-in-Publication Data

Macdonald, Fiona.
   A 16th century mosque / Fiona Macdonald, Mark Bergin.
      p.   cm. — (Inside story)
   Includes index.
   ISBN 0-87226-310-X
   1. Mosques—Juvenile literature.   2. Süleymaniye Camil (Istanbul, Turkey)—Juvenile literature.   [1. Mosques.   2. Islam.]
   I. Bergin, Mark.   II. Title.   III. Title: Sixteenth century mosque.
   IV. Series: Inside story (Peter Bedrick Books)
   BP187.62.M33   1994
   297'.65—dc20   94–20008
                                                    CIP

Printed and bound in Hong Kong by Wing King Tong Ltd.
10 9 8 7 6 5 4 3 2 1

INSIDE STORY

A 16th CENTURY MOSQUE

FIONA MACDONALD   MARK BERGIN

PETER BEDRICK BOOKS

NEW YORK

CONTENTS

INTRODUCTION

All over the world, splendid mosques stand proudly at the heart of many cities and towns. They proclaim, first and foremost, their communities' Islamic faith. They also display the prosperity and artistic taste of the men and women who commissioned architects and builders to construct them.

Many people think that the sixteenth-century mosques in and around the great city of Istanbul are among the most beautiful ever built. With their enormous domed roofs and spectacularly tall minarets (towers), they were technically very advanced for their time. They have also been praised for their elegance, lightness and grace.

Most of these lovely buildings were designed for Sultan Suleyman the Magnificent, ruler of the mighty Ottoman empire, by the architect Sinan Pasha (1491-1588). In this book, we will look at Sinan's long and brilliant career at Suleyman's court, and at the beautiful mosques he built. They are still admired today as some of the finest achievements of Islamic art.

EUROPE

BALKANS

ITALY

Rome

GREECE

Byzantium

SPAIN

Mediterranean Sea

Cordova

Seville

Alexandria

MUSLIM LANDS AROUND **AD 950**

Cairo

EGYPT

AFRICA

THE SPREAD OF ISLAM

The Prophet Muhammad was born in Mecca, Arabia, around AD 570. After his parents died, he was brought up by his grandfather, guardian of a shrine called Kaaba.

As a young man, Muhammad did not share his grandfather's religious concerns. Instead, he worked with his uncle, a traveling merchant. In AD 595, he became a merchant himself. Muhammad was successful, but he was worried by the greed and cruelty he saw all around. So he took time off in the mountains, to think and meditate. There, in AD 610, he had the first of several revelations. At first, he was frightened by them, but, gradually, he came to believe that they were messages sent by God. These messages formed the basis of the faith called 'Islam'.

In AD 613, encouraged by his wife Khadijah, Muhammad began to preach. He told the citizens of Mecca about God's messages, and urged them to lead better lives. They became angry and hostile, so, in AD 622, Muhammad moved to Medina. A few Meccans went with him. Together, they formed the first community of Muslims – people who follow the faith of Islam.

As the Muslim community in Medina grew, they felt strong enough to fight to defend their faith. By 630, they captured Mecca. Muhammad was welcomed back, and re-dedicated Kaaba as a center of Muslim worship. Muhammad died in 632, but the Islamic faith he had preached quickly spread, through trade and conquest, across Africa, Asia and the Middle East.

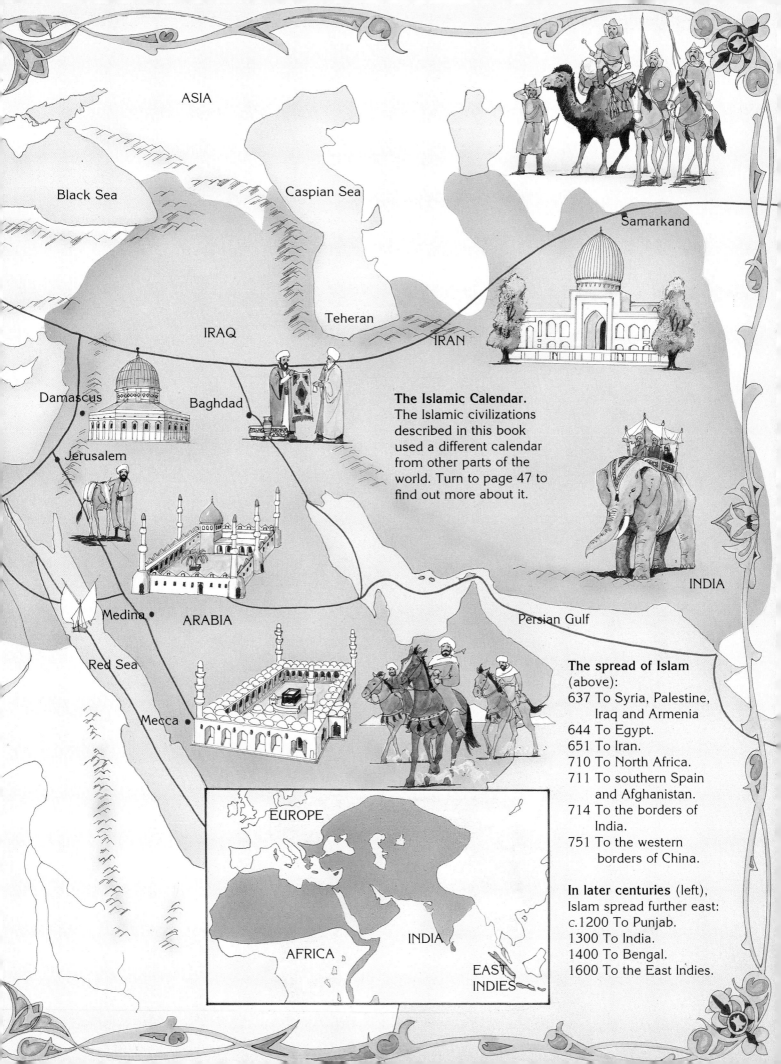

ASIA

Black Sea

Caspian Sea

Samarkand

Teheran

IRAQ

IRAN

Damascus

Baghdad

Jerusalem

The Islamic Calendar.
The Islamic civilizations
described in this book
used a different calendar
from other parts of the
world. Turn to page 47 to
find out more about it.

INDIA

Medina

ARABIA

Red Sea

Persian Gulf

Mecca

The spread of Islam
(above):
637 To Syria, Palestine,
     Iraq and Armenia
644 To Egypt.
651 To Iran.
710 To North Africa.
711 To southern Spain
     and Afghanistan.
714 To the borders of
     India.
751 To the western
     borders of China.

In later centuries (left),
Islam spread further east:
c.1200 To Punjab.
1300 To India.
1400 To Bengal.
1600 To the East Indies.

EUROPE

AFRICA

INDIA

EAST
INDIES

THE ISLAMIC FAITH

1 2 3 4 5

Muslims were encouraged to pray five times a day. Before each prayer, Muslims washed to purify their bodies. Then they turned to face Mecca and performed several 'rakats' of prayer: reciting verses from the Qur'an while making a sequence of movements showing obedience and devotion to God.

Movements for prayer:
(1) Proclaiming 'Allahu Akbar' (God is most great). (2) Bowing. (3) Kneeling. (4) Bending low. (5) Looking right and left to say 'Peace and God's mercy be with you.' Stages (3) and (4) are repeated twice.

What did the first Muslims believe? The essence of Islam was summed up in words known as the 'shahada' (witness or testimony). They proclaimed: 'There is no God but Allah [the Arabic word for God], and Muhammad is the messenger of God'. Anyone who spoke the words of the shahada, honestly and sincerely, identified themself as a Muslim.

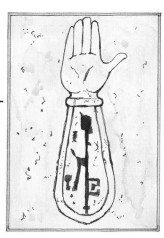

Medieval Spanish carving symbolizing the Five Pillars of Islam.

Money collected as Zakat (charity) might be given to poor people, or used for community projects such as building schools and hospitals or providing fresh water supplies.

Religion – any religion – involves more than belief. The way people worship and the way they behave are also very important. Muslims aimed to integrate their faith with their everyday lives. So Muslims were expected to have faith, to pray regularly, to give to charity, to fast (go without food and drink) and to make a pilgrimage to the holy city of Mecca.

Taken together, these five key elements of Muslim life were sometimes known as the 'Five Pillars' of Islam. They supported Muslims by helping them maintain their faith and live in a way they hoped would please God.

They helped in other ways, too. Praying in public, giving and receiving charity, the shared experience of fasting, and traveling together on pilgrimage all helped encourage friendship and co-operation between members of the Muslim community in the Muslim homeland of Arabia and throughout the world.

Pilgrimage was a solemn but joyful occasion – Muslims were traveling (as one historian has described it) 'to present themselves to God.'

Going on pilgrimage might involve a long, dangerous journey through rough country. Rich Muslims gave money to build resthouses and dig wells along busy pilgrim routes. As pilgrims reached Mecca, they changed into simple white clothes (to show humility). They walked 7 times around Kaaba (the building where, Muslims believe, God was first worshipped) and took part in other holy ceremonies.

THE FIRST MOSQUE

Wealthy Arabian merchants lived in homes like this: low, single-story buildings with private family rooms, workrooms, living quarters for slaves, storerooms, and stabling for camels. Traders might set up stalls in the shelter of the courtyard wall and nomad families might pitch their tents nearby.

In 622, when Muhammad went to Medina, there was no suitable building where they could meet and worship. So they gathered in Muhammad's house, to listen to him preaching and to pray. Eventually, Muhammad's house became known as a 'masjid' – a place where people bow down. All later 'masjids' (mosques) have developed from this simple beginning.

We do not know what the first mosque looked like, but it was probably similar to other homes in Arabia, with a shady courtyard where family and friends could meet. Close by, outside, were shops, stalls and busy streets. The first mosque lay at the heart of the first Muslim town.

Muhammad always insisted that the message he preached – in the mosque or elsewhere – came from God. After his death, this message was preserved in a book known as the Qur'an.

Few people in 7th-century Arabia could read and write, and the complete text of the Qur'an was not finalized until after Muhammad's death. But some of his preaching was noted on scraps of palm-leaf by people who listened to him. The rest was memorized by members of early Muslim communities, and passed on from generation to generation. In the same way, many of Muhammad's own sayings were remembered and preserved as 'hadith' (traditions).

Shops (above) in a busy town in 13th-century Iran. Left to right: jeweler, apothecary, butcher, baker. Some cities banned the sale of smelly goods, such as cooking oil, close to their mosques. Medieval Muslims were enterprising merchants and traders. Success in business was welcomed as a sign of God's favor.

Mosques were built in cities and villages throughout the Muslim world. They were holy places, but they were not cut off from the rest of the world. Booths for scribes, and hospitals and schools might be built nearby. For a Muslim, religion was part of everyday life. There was no gap between 'holy' and 'unholy' things – God saw and judged all thoughts and actions. Religious laws governed everything from fair trading and paying taxes to caring for children or going to war.

SIMPLE OR ELABORATE STYLES

A mosque in the desert near Aden, built of stone and sun-dried mud bricks, and roofed with palm leaf thatch. Simple, local mosques have been built to traditional designs like this for hundreds of years.

As the faith of Islam spread through many lands, kings, government officials and other wealthy Muslims gave money so that mosques could be built for believers to meet in and pray together. All these mosques had similar features, because they were designed to provide what was needed for worship. They had somewhere for people to wash before praying, and to leave their dirty shoes. They had a special niche in one wall which showed the direction of Mecca, so worshippers knew which way to face when they prayed. Inside there was a large open space, often roofed over, where people could kneel side by side. And there was usually a pulpit where the prayer-leader could stand to be seen and heard.

However, from the outside, mosques did not all look the same. They varied from plain, single story constructions to huge complexes with courtyards and towers, gateways and domes. Building materials and styles varied from place to place. Mosques also became more elaborate as building techniques developed over the years. The simplest mosques were built in desert regions where bricks and stone were scarce, and where there was no local tradition of building. (Many desert peoples were nomads, who lived in tents.) Bigger, grander mosques were built in busy cities where there was a large Muslim population – and local expertise in designing complicated buildings for inner-city sites.

The Great Mosque (right), Qairawan, Tunisia, built in 836 on the site of an earlier mosque. It is the oldest surviving mosque in North Africa.

prayer hall

minaret

courtyard

Close-up (left) of tiles at the Royal Mosque, Isfahan. Following Muslim tradition, only abstract patterns were used for decoration; 7 brilliant colors were combined in elaborate designs. Many Muslims believed it was wrong to paint people or animals, because only God could create life.

Magnificent gateway (right) to the prayer hall of the Royal Mosque at Isfahan, Iran, built 1612–1613. It is 89 feet high and decorated with beautiful colored tiles, which was

a traditional way of ornamenting important buildings in Iran and Central Asia. The city of Isfahan was rebuilt as his capital by powerful Shah Abbas I, who ruled from 1588 to 1629.

WORKERS' LIVES

Apart from royal palaces, mosques were usually the biggest and most important buildings in any Muslim community. No one built taller or more magnificent structures until the nineteenth and twentieth centuries. In busy towns and cities, they were an easily-recognizable sign of prosperity and rank. Generally speaking, the bigger and more important a city, the bigger and more important its mosque. Individuals or groups who paid for a mosque also wanted it to reflect their good taste – as well as their respect and devotion to the faith of Islam.

Before sunrise. Time to get up, dressed and ready for work. Morning prayers.

A DAY IN THE LIFE OF A MASON

7:00 am (summer), Breakfast time: bread and yogurt served by wife or servant. Water to drink.

7:30 am Walks to building site past craftsmen's stalls. City laws say that only properly-trained craftsmen should work.

8:00 am Foreman gives orders. As in many Muslim lands, people of different faiths work well together.

10:00 am A load of tiles has arrived from the kiln. Supervises the slaves who are unloading them.

3:00 pm (above) After a rest during mid-day heat, works with other masons building arches to support roof.
6:00 pm (left) After prayer, walks home through market. Buys lamb and onions for wife to cook.

Mid-day prayers. Lunch (bread and cheese), then watches and admires the master tiler at work (right).

grooves collect rainwater

women's private rooms

courtyard

flat roof for extra living space

small barred windows

thick walls

Late medieval house from Muslim southern Spain. Houses similar to this were built in many Muslim lands, providing privacy and security for families and servants.

9:00 pm Entertains male friends to dinner; they eat spicy stew and drink coffee.

In many lands, Muslim women were encouraged to stay at home. But they still worked: poor women and female slaves cooked, spun thread, nursed the sick and cared for children. Rich women became scholars.

Most of the craft workers who built mosques were Muslims – but not all. It depended where the mosque was sited. In some Muslim lands – Spain, North Africa, the Middle East - non-Muslim workers were employed, because they were trained in particular skills, for example, plasterwork. To Muslims, Christians and Jews were both 'peoples of the book', that is, they worshipped the same God as Muslims, and shared many important religious teachings, as recorded in the Bible. So Jews and Christians were given special 'dhimmi' or 'protected minority' status in Muslim cities, although they did not share equal civil rights. The different communities lived, prayed, and trained as craftsmen (women did not build), separately but peacefully, on the whole.

THE OTTOMAN EMPIRE

The Ottoman Empire
(right) during the reign of
Sultan (emperor)
Suleyman II 'the
Magnificent' (or 'the
Lawgiver'), 1520-1566.

People of the Empire:
1. Wealthy Turkish
   woman and daughter.
2. Mameluke woman
   from Egypt.
3. Servant.
4. Christian merchant
   from Bosnia.
5. Jewish doctor.
6. Syrian woman.
7. Sufi (Muslim mystic).
8. Turkish kebab-seller.
9. Turkish water-carrier.

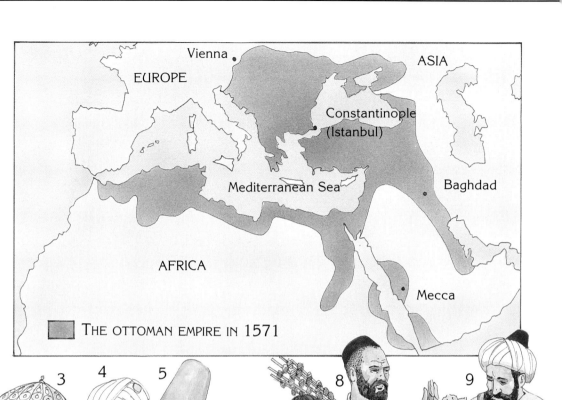

THE OTTOMAN EMPIRE IN 1571

The people on these
pages were first
portrayed by a French
traveler in 1568.

Merchant

Qadi

1

2

3

A merchant from Arabia. Muslim merchants traveled to many different lands.

A Qadi, or scholar who was expert in Islamic law. Islamic law – called 'Sharia' - was based on the Qur'an. Qadis acted as judges in the Islamic courts.

Ottoman Troops: (1) Turkish Siphai, or cavalry soldier. (2) Trainee Janissary. (3) Janissary soldier in parade uniform. The 30,000 Janissaries were elite troops recruited from Christian boy slaves sent to the Empire by conquered lands.

As the Islamic faith spread rapidly, a powerful, brilliant Muslim civilization developed. Lands under Muslim control in southern Europe, North Africa, Asia and the Middle East were ruled by caliphs, leaders with political and religious powers. At first, the caliphs governed from Damascus in Syria, but in 762 they moved to a new capital city at Baghdad in Iraq.

Baghdad was the center of Muslim civilization for many years, though other Muslim rulers often ignored the caliphs' powers. But in 1258, Baghdad was destroyed by Mongol invaders. For a while, some Muslim lands had no strong government. But ambitious new Muslim states soon grew up,

eager to defend Islam against fresh Mongol raids and against Christian crusaders from the west.

The strongest and most energetic of these new states was founded by a Turk called Osman – 'Ottoman' in English – who ruled from 1281-1324. Later Ottoman sultans (rulers) fought tirelessly to win new lands. In 1453, sultan Mehmet 'the Conqueror' captured Constantinople. He re-named it Istanbul, and it became the stronghold of the Byzantine empire. By the sixteenth century, the Ottomans were the most powerful rulers in the Middle East, and strong enough to fight off rival Muslim states in Egypt and Iran, as well as a huge Christian battle-fleet.

SULEYMAN THE MAGNIFICENT

Sultan Suleyman II was born in 1494, and came to the throne in 1520. During his reign, Ottoman power was at its height. For many years, his empire was at war – he fought against Iran and conquered Hungary; his generals led campaigns in India, Arabia, Egypt and North Africa; his ships clashed with French and Italian fleets in the Mediterranean. He died in Hungary in 1566.

In Europe, he was known as 'Suleyman the Magnificent' – a tribute to the splendor and brilliance of his court. A French traveler wrote in 1554: 'he sat on cushions made of cloth of gold. He wore a robe of white satin, and a turban over a cap of deep red velvet. A round gold brooch set with a glittering ruby, large as a hazel-nut, was pinned to the turban.'

Suleyman's Ottoman subjects called him 'the Lawgiver'; he made firm laws and employed good administrators to bring stability to Ottoman lands. Sharia (Islamic law) was enforced, too.

For nearly 30 years, Suleyman worked with the architect Sinan Pasha (1491-1588) to transform Constantinople with fine new buildings. Like many of Suleyman's top officials, Sinan was recruited through the 'devshirme' system: boys from conquered countries were taken to serve as soldiers or slaves. This system was not new, but Suleyman used it wisely.

The Ottoman sultans ruled from a magnificent palace, the Topkapi Serai, in the center of Istanbul. Outside, it looked unremarkable, but inside it was a treasure-house of colored tiles, silken carpets, glittering glass, metalwork and jewelery.

Mirror (right, top) made for Suleyman II, 1543-1544. The handle is ebony and the frame is carved ivory. Sword (right, below) in a jewel-studded gold scabbard, also made for Suleyman II. The Ottoman sultans paid craftsmen to make lamps, flasks, caskets, turban-pins and even armor from precious metals and stones.

Sultan Suleyman II's ceremonial signature (below), called a 'tughra'. Scribes arranged the letters of Suleyman's name in an elaborate pattern which was written at the bottom of all his government's official documents, to authorize them. Suleyman was a talented scribe; he was reported to have copied out the words of the entire Qur'an 8 times. This was a religious action, as well as a display of his artistic skill.

DOMED ROOFS

Sinan Pasha was appointed Court Architect in 1538. Before that, he worked as an army engineer for many years. It was said that Suleyman first noticed Sinan's skills during the battle campaigns of the 1530s, when Sinan built a bridge to a revolutionary design.

Sinan was born in Turkey, to a Greek Orthodox Christian family. In Turkey, ancient temples and medieval churches were all around. He observed many local building styles as he traveled to the wars. As Court Architect, he could consult Suleyman's fine library, which contained many books on architecture and history. He may also have met European artists who told him about new, Renaissance designs.

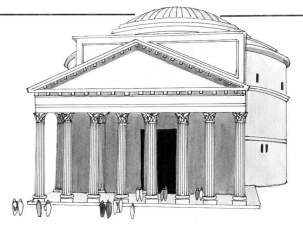

The Pantheon (above) in Rome, built AD 100-125, was the largest domed building in the ancient world. The dome was 140 feet in diameter.

The Pantheon dome (below) was built of brick and concrete It was supported by drum-shaped walls, made of rows of columns.

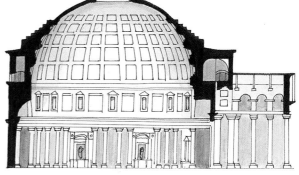

The Great Mosque in Damascus, Syria, built 705-715. Its design was based on earlier Christian churches. It was decorated with beautiful Islamic mosaics, showing trees and abstract patterns.

The tall minaret (tower used by an announcer, or Muezzin, to call Muslims to prayer) at the mosque in Samarra, Iraq. Samarra was built around 836 as a new town to house the bodyguards of the Abbasid ruling dynasty. The Abbasids came to power in 750 as caliphs (leaders of the Muslim world). Islamic arts and sciences flourished under their rule.

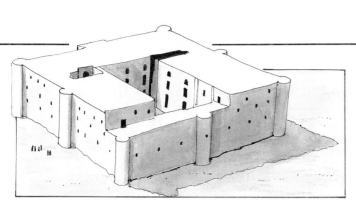

Sinan used all this information when planning his own buildings. He also used his engineering experience to try and solve a major technical problem. How could he cover the wide open space of a mosque prayer hall with a graceful and elegant roof? The answer was with a dome.

The Romans had built domed temples, but they were round. This was not a suitable shape for Muslim worship: people knelt side by side, all facing Mecca, to say their prayers. A few early Islamic buildings had small domes. Technically, the greatest breakthrough had been made by Christian architects at a church called the Holy Wisdom. They had found a way of building a dome on top of a big, square hall. Sinan wanted to do even better, for the glory of Islam.

Islamic architecture (above, left): an 8th-century palace in the desert in Jordan. It was built round a courtyard, used for meetings and prayers.

The Dome of the Rock, Jerusalem (above), built as a Muslim shrine between 687-691. It combined Roman and Islamic architectural styles.

buttress – supports weight of dome

dome

pendentive

square nave

A dome can be supported on top of a square building by constructing shapes known as pendentives, colored pink here.

pendentive

dome

square building

Right and below:
The church of the Holy Wisdom in Constantinople, built AD 532-537

dome

square nave

buttress

A MOSQUE FOR SULEYMAN

The beautiful domed church of the Holy Wisdom stood right in the center of **Constantinople**. When the Ottomans captured the city in 1453, they turned the church into a mosque. But that was not good enough for Sinan or Suleyman. They wanted to build magnificent mosques of their own.

It was a proud tradition among rich Muslim families to give money to pay for religious buildings of all kinds. Since becoming Court Architect, Sinan had already designed a mosque (the Shehzade, built 1544-1548) in memory of one of Suleyman's sons. Other important figures at the Ottoman court also asked Sinan to work for them; he built mosques for two of Suleyman's most powerful government officials, Sokullu Mehmed Pasha and Rustem Pasha, and also for Suleyman's daughter, Princess Mirimah.

In 1550, Suleyman told Sinan that he wanted a mosque as his own memorial. Sinan's task was to design a building – the Suleymaniye mosque – that would be a peaceful place of worship but would also reflect Suleyman's splendor and artistic tastes. Sinan hoped it would be technically more advanced, too.

The Suleymaniye mosque, Constantinople:

1. Crescent – a symbol of Islam.
2. Dome.
3. Minaret .
4. Flying buttress.
5. Pendentive (stonework built to support a circular dome on top of a square frame formed by four massive pillars at the corners of the prayer-hall. One pillar, labeled 11, is visible in the drawing opposite).
6. Round plaque with inscription from the Qur'an.
7. Brick and stone arch.
8. Towers and buttresses, support the weight of the dome. The towers are topped with umbrella-shaped roofs. Together, towers and buttresses stop the weight of the dome pushing the walls of the prayer-hall outwards. Without them, the mosque would collapse.
9. Huge arched window.
10. Buttress supporting outer walls of prayer-hall
11. Pier (pillar helping to support the dome).
12. Lamplighter's gallery, made of decorative ironwork.
13. Prayer-hall floor, covered with carpets.
14. Courtyard.
15. Main gateway.
16. Qibla wall, containing a niche (mihrab) showing worshippers the direction of Mecca.

The mosque was designed as a traditional group or 'complex': a courtyard and a prayer-hall plus many other buildings designed to benefit the community. Because of its central site, shops and newly-fashionable coffee houses were built along one outer wall.

1

2

3

4

5

6

7

8

9

10

11

12

13

16

direction of Mecca

A DIFFICULT TASK

Sinan and his team of workmen finished the Suleymaniye mosque and all its associated buildings in less than seven years, between 1550-1557. This was an astonishing achievement; the mosque, its courtyard and small royal cemetery next door covered a huge area – almost 324,000 square feet. In addition, the hospital, soup kitchen, schools, guesthouse and baths belonging to the mosque covered an equally large plot of land.

Sinan's task was made all the more difficult by the site Suleyman chose for his new mosque. He wanted it built in the gardens of the old royal palace – a beautiful hillside with views over the narrow strip of sea called the Golden Horn, which separates the continents of Europe and Asia. But the gardens were rocky and steep, so Sinan had to build a vast platform to provide a secure foundation for the mosque before any construction work could start. He also built a small house for himself nearby, so he would be available night and day in order to supervise the work.

Sinan's third main problem was pressure from Suleyman to finish 'his' mosque quickly. The emperor was getting old (he was 56 in 1550; Sinan was 59), and he was unwell. He wanted to see the building complete before he died. In fact, Suleyman lived for almost ten years after his mosque was officially opened in 1557.

The Suleymaniye mosque was built of honey-colored stone and grey marble, with smaller amounts of rare green, red or white marble used for decoration. Some of the stonework was originally painted blue, but Sinan seems to have changed his mind, and suggested black, red and white paints instead. Hasan Çelebi, a famous calligrapher from Circassia (on the borders of present-day Russia and Georgia), carved and painted most of the inscriptions that decorate the mosque. Round the inside of the great dome, lit by 32 windows, he wrote a verse from the Qur'an: 'God is the light of the heavens and the earth.'

Building the Suleymaniye mosque cost an enormous amount of money. Sinan and Emperor Suleyman both insisted that only the best materials and the best workmen were used. They were brought to Constantinople from distant parts of the Ottoman Empire if necessary.

Sinan's chief clerk came from Armenia. He kept careful, detailed accounts of all the money spent of the great new building, using his own Armenian language, not the official Ottoman Turkish spoken and written at Suleyman's court.

THE CALL TO PRAYER

The Suleymaniye mosque's sloping site meant that the whole building complex loomed over the city's busy streets. This was deliberate. Sinan and Suleyman wanted it to be an unmistakable sign of the greatness of Islam – and of the power of the Ottoman Empire, as well.

Many other features made the Suleymaniye mosque impressive. Four towering minarets stood at the corners of its courtyard (only royal buildings could have more than one), and rows of small domes decorated the courtyard roof. Altogether, Sinan used over 400 small domes to decorate the mosque. They created a dramatic pattern against the sky, and echoed the towering bulk of the prayer-hall's main dome.

At the Suleymaniye mosque, Sinan did not succeed in his aim of building a dome that was wider and higher than the church of the Holy Wisdom. But he did create a wonderfully light and spacious prayer-hall, surrounded by a cluster of sturdy smaller buildings. He also designed two elegant türbe (small buildings, used as tombs) where Suleyman and his favorite wife, Hürrem Sultan, were buried. Sinan's own tomb was built nearby.

There are four minarets (two tall and two small) at the Suleymaniye mosque. The two tallest are 210 feet high, excluding the pointed lead roofs on top.

Muezzin

balcony

Golden Horn

main gate

Muezzins recited these words when calling people to prayer:
In the name of God, the merciful, the compassionate.
God is most great.
I witness that there is no god but God.
I witness that Muhammad is God's Prophet.
Come to prayers.
Come and be saved.
God is most great.
There is no god but God.

Minarets (left) were built in many local styles. The higher they were, the further the Muezzin's call would carry:
1. Delhi, India;
2. Tunis, north Africa;
3. Cairo, Egypt.
If there was no minaret, Muezzins called from roofs or high walls.

1   2   3

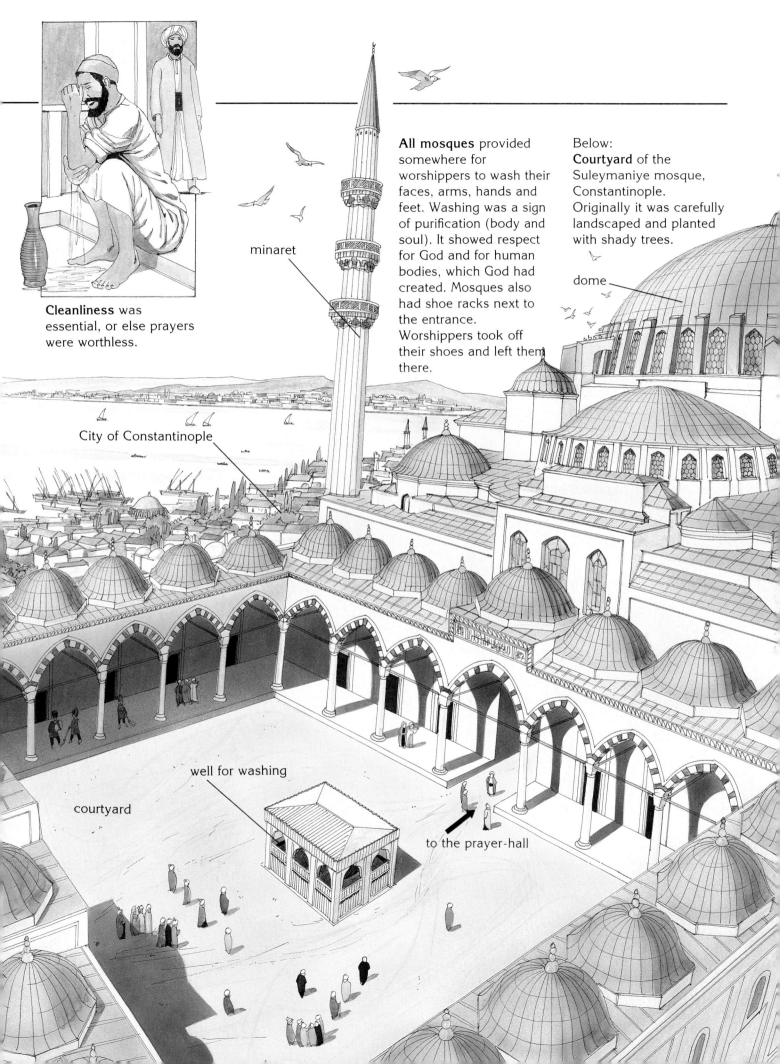

Cleanliness was essential, or else prayers were worthless.

minaret

All mosques provided somewhere for worshippers to wash their faces, arms, hands and feet. Washing was a sign of purification (body and soul). It showed respect for God and for human bodies, which God had created. Mosques also had shoe racks next to the entrance. Worshippers took off their shoes and left them there.

Below:
Courtyard of the Suleymaniye mosque, Constantinople. Originally it was carefully landscaped and planted with shady trees.

dome

City of Constantinople

well for washing

courtyard

to the prayer-hall

MIHRAB AND MINBAR

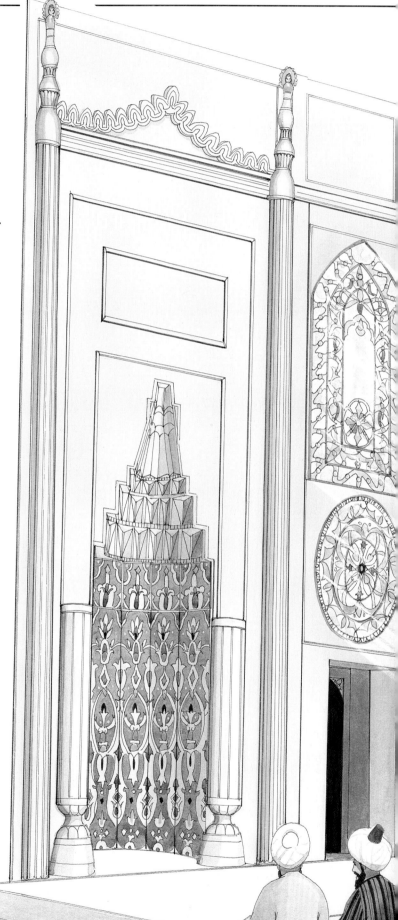

The first worshippers came to the Suleymaniye mosque to pray and to listen to sermons in 1557. They quickly discovered that the inside of the mosque was just as impressive as the outside. The focus of their assembly – the holy direction of Mecca – was marked by a splendid mihrab, or niche, set into one wall. This grey marble mihrab was decorated with the finest green and gold calligraphy that Sinan could obtain. On either side stood a tall, elegant marble column.

To Suleyman, Sinan, the craftworkers, and the worshippers at the mosque, the beautiful mihrab showed their reverence for the city of Mecca where the Prophet Muhammad had lived, and where, they believed, God had first been worshipped long ago at the ancient Kaaba.

Next to the mihrab, Sinan designed a tall minbar, or pulpit, where the Imam of the mosque stood to preach at Friday prayers. Muslim traditions told how the stepped minbar shape had developed from the simple ladder that Muhammad climbed when preaching, so that more people could hear him. The Suleymaniye minbar was made of carved marble, patterned in green and white. The dark blue spire at the top was decorated with golden stars, like the night sky.

Scene inside a mosque (left), from a 13th-century Iranian manuscript. An Imam is preaching to worshippers seated on the floor.

Mihrabs (right) were usually decorated with stone or plaster carvings, mosaics, or tiles. Tall candles might be placed on either side; there are huge candle-holders in the Suleymaniye mosque.

fountain

courtyard

mihrab

minbar

Plan (above) of a typical mosque. However different they looked outside, most mosques contained these features.

dikka

Platform (above), called a dikka, where the Qaris (or sometimes the Muezzins) stood to repeat the words of the Imam as he led the Friday prayers.

kursi

Kursi (reading stand) (left), to hold a copy of the Qur'an. A mosque official called a Qari, with a clear, pleasant voice, read from the Qur'an during prayers.

mihrab

minbar

direction of Mecca

dikka

kursi

typical layout

To give his sermon, the Imam climbed into the minbar, or pulpit. Being high up helped his voice carry to the back of the mosque. Originally, minbars were small and simple, but by Ottoman times, they were

designed in elaborate styles. The Imam never preached from the top: Islamic tradition taught that only the Prophet Muhammad did. Imams preached from further down.

CARVINGS AND TILES

Although Sinan had not trained in Suleyman's palace schools, he was an expert manager. As well as designing his great mosques, he also needed to coordinate a large workforce of specialist craftsmen. These workers were highly trained; many belonged to guilds, which inspected members' work to ensure high standards. Ottoman skills included metalwork, wood-carving and stone-carving. All these techniques were used to decorate the Sulyemaniye mosque. Doors, windows and screens were carved with intricate patterns. Many were traditional, and most were based on mathematical shapes. It was particularly important for a mosque to have a beautiful door. It reminded worshippers that regular prayer and readings from the Qur'an were spiritual 'doorways', leading to God.

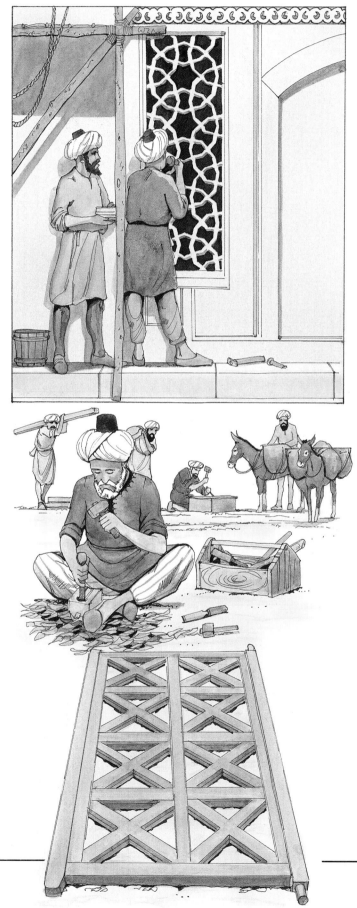

Stone carvers at work (right) creating an abstract design.

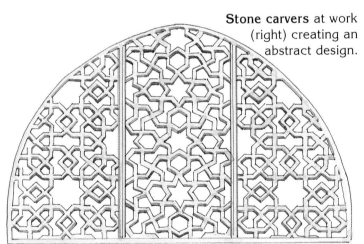

Fragile glass windows (above) in their plasterwork frames were protected by decorative grilles, made of iron or stone. Spaces above windows and gateways were also filled with elaborately patterned carvings. This stone grille is from the Shehzade Mehmet mosque in Constantinople, designed by Sinan between 1544 and 1548.

Mosque doors (right) were made of wood, carved (using a mallet and chisel) with geometric patterns or with inscriptions from the Qur'an. The doors of the Suleymaniye mosque were inlaid with ivory, ebony and mother of pearl – this was very highly valued in 16th-century Turkey. Latches and hinges were usually made of bronze.

Tiles (left) patterned with inscriptions from the Qur'an, used to decorate the mihrab at the Suleymaniye mosque. Below: tiles were painted with chemical mixtures, using a fine brush. Then they were fired (heated) in a kiln. It took great skill to get the right temperature. If it was too hot or too cold, the tiles would be ruined.

The most famous Ottoman craftworkers were the tile-makers who worked at Iznik, in Turkey. During Suleyman's reign, they invented a way of painting tiles using bright colors (green, purple, blue, lilac, red, white and black) covered by a shiny, transparent glaze. Favorite designs were based on flowers; carnations were especially popular. Suleyman's Topkapi palace, his tomb, and many mosques were decorated like this. The Sultan Ahmed mosque in Constantinople contained 20,000 tiles.

Tiles were usually painted, but small pieces cut from colored tiles could also be arranged to make mosaics. These tile mosaics were invented by craftworkers in Iran around 1200.

CARPETS AND RUGS

Finished cloth (far left) and yarns for weaving were dyed in clay-lined pits. Dyes were smelly and messy.
A chemist's shop (left) in 14th-century Iraq. Dyes were made from plants, mixed with chemicals like salt or alum to 'fix' them.

The ancestors of the Ottoman Sultans were nomads – warriors and herdsmen who rode across the dry, dusty grasslands of Central Asia before settling in Turkey with their flocks of sheep and herds of goats. While the nomadic Turkish men hunted and fought and looked after their animals, their wives and daughters spun sheeps' wool and goat-hair to make yarn, and wove cloth to make tents, saddlebags and clothes for their families. Some discovered how to make dyes from wild plants.

Turkish women – like nomad women in other Muslim lands – also made carpets and rugs. Carpets originated as floor-coverings for tents. They were soft, warm and easy to pack up (usually women's work) when a nomad family moved camp. They were also a way of displaying a family's wealth.

Before long, merchants traveled out from the towns to buy carpets made by nomads, and a profitable industry began. The best carpets, brightly patterned and with a smooth, lustrous pile, were highly prized and were purchased for large sums by wealthy Ottoman citizens. Sultan Suleyman's palace was furnished with wonderful carpets, many in a special 'Ottoman' design. Carpets were also used to cover the floor in mosques, as a sign of respect; they showed the ground was dedicated to God.

Women and children were trained to make carpets, because their small hands could tie finer knots.

Carpets were woven from wool, cotton or silk. Below: carpet-makers' tools. 1. knives for cutting knots. 2. comb for pressing knots together. 3. shears for trimming pile.

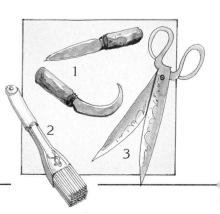

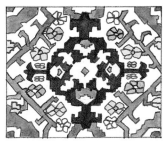

Floral designs originated at the Ottoman court and were widely copied.

Border pattern from a kilim rug – a simpler, cheaper type of carpet.

16th-century carpet pattern based on a rose ('gul' in Turkish).

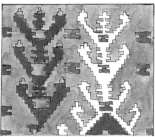

Pattern from a kilim rug based on plants and trees.

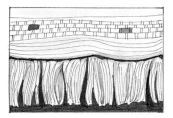

Most carpets were trimmed with a fringe at each end.

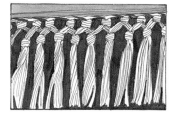

This was made by knotting warp threads together.

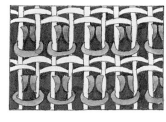

Persian knot, used in Iran, Central Asia and China.

Merchants (left) sold carpets in the busy city of Constantinople. Turkish and Persian carpets were prized worldwide.

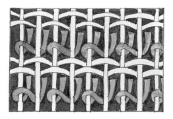

Ghiordes knot, used in most Turkish carpets.

Many carpets were produced in 'prayer rug' style (below), with a design showing a mihrab. They were used by Muslims for daily prayers.

LIGHT AND COLOR

furnace

sand, heated with soda to make glass

hollow tube

glass bubble

hollow wooden mold

Glass blowers at work in 16th-century Constantinople. They are working next to a furnace containing red-hot molten glass. Each blower picks up a blob of molten glass on the end of a long metal tube. Then he blows very hard, to create a thin 'bubble' of glass. As the glass cools, it solidifies in the shape he has blown. Glass made like this was precious, and was used for lamps, flagons and mosque windows.

Fine Iznik pottery (below), produced in Ottoman Turkey: 1. Vase; 2. Dish; 3. Mosque lamp. This lamp held a small container with a wick for burning oil. It needed to be trimmed regularly to stop it smoking.

Sinan designed the domed roofs of his mosques with many windows, so that daylight would shine down on people at prayer, like a blessing from God. But at certain seasons and, obviously, after sunset, natural light was not enough. So oil lamps were suspended on metal chains from mosque ceilings, and lamplighters were employed to keep them filled. Sinan built a special gallery around the dome at the Suleymaniye mosque, so that lamplighters could reach the hundreds of hanging lamps.

Traditionally, the finest mosque lamps were made of glass or crystal, inscribed with words from the Qur'an. But only wealthy mosques could afford these. Most had lamps made of pottery. They provided light but were not very pretty. In the sixteenth century, potters began to make fine ceramic lamps.

Glassworkers and metalworkers collaborated to produce stained-glass windows; metalworkers also made bronze locks and hinges for the mosque doors. The glass for the windows at the Suleymaniye mosque was made by Ibrahim Sarhosh (Ibrahim the Drunkard). Normally, Muslims were forbidden to drink alcohol, but Ibrahim's work was so good that Suleyman did not punish him. Many of the mosque's windows are double – the fine glass inside is protected by a screen.

Islamic metalwork (left). The best came from Mosul in Iraq. Objects like these, made between 1200-1500, were treasured at Ottoman royal courts.
1. Brass incense-burner with engraved patterns.
2. Bronze aquamanile – jug in animal shape
3. Brass candlestick. Candles were also used to light mosques.

Glaziers at work, making stained glass windows for a mosque. Small pieces of colored glass were held together by lead strips.

Cheap, everyday craft goods (below), like baskets and cooking pots, were sold in shops near the Suleymaniye mosque.

PEOPLE OF THE MOSQUE

People who might be involved in the decision to build a new mosque:
1. Qadi.
2. Religious scholar.
3. Community elder.
4. Imam.
5. Architect.
6. Wealthy donor.

Ottoman sultans gave money to build many fine mosques throughout their empire. Suleyman II was keenly interested in architecture. He had already commissioned major projects in the holy cities of Mecca and Jerusalem before he employed Sinan in Constantinople.

Wherever mosques were built – in capital cities (like the Suleymaniye) or in remote villages – they became centers of local communities. As well as being places of prayer, they were also places where friends and neighbors met at least once a week, and where many people worked.

Local issues were often discussed by community elders at the end of Friday prayers; they might seek guidance from the Imam, or, if complicated matters of law were involved, from a Qadi. Even in the Ottoman empire, which had a system of strong laws, Sharia (Islamic law) was still the most important. It regulated people's private lives – child care, divorce, inheritance – as well as community business. In many parts of the empire, local customs and traditions also shaped community life.

Like any buildings, mosques had to be cared for, cleaned and repaired by a staff of sweepers and caretakers. Teachers and scribes might also be employed.

Men learned in Islamic law formed a respected group in the community, known as the Ulama. In Suleyman's reign, they played an important part in government and education.

Larger mosques had medreses (colleges) built nearby. There, teachers and pupils studied the Qur'an, Islamic law, mathematics, medicine and philosophy.

Muslim men went to their town's main mosque for communal prayers every Friday at noon. Muslim men might also meet during the week to study the Qur'an or to listen to the words of a wandering sufi (a Muslim mystic). In many countries, women stayed at home to pray.

But if local tradition allowed them to go the mosque, they sat separately from the men, in a private gallery or behind screens. After prayers, everyone listened to a sermon from the Imam. It was based on words of the Qur'an.

Mosques employed a large staff to sweep the floors, fill the oil lamps and carry out repairs.

The Muezzin called Muslims to prayer. At dawn he reminded them, 'Prayer is better than sleep.'

SCHOOLS AND COLLEGES

Young boys attended primary school at the Suleymaniye mosque. They learned about Islam and were taught to recite passages from the Qur'an. (These were in Arabic, so boys also had to learn to translate them.) Teachers hoped pupils would remember these holy words for the rest of their lives, and that they would help them to live as good Muslims. The text of the Qur'an was also loved and admired as beautiful poetry.

Clever boys might be taught to read and write Arabic, so they could study the Qur'an and books written by leading Muslim scholars. They learned to read and write their own language, as well. If a boy was a really good student, he might win a place at a medrese (college). There he could study philosophy, science, medicine or law.

There were four grades of medrese in the Ottoman empire; students who graduated from the lower grades became scribes, lawyers or civil servants. Outstanding students, who graduated from the top grade, became medrese teachers themselves, or senior Qadis. The four best medreses in Constantinople were built by Sinan, next door to the Suleymaniye mosque, which became a great center of learning.

Girls did not usually attend schools or colleges; their parents, private tutors or well-educated slaves taught them at home.

In some Muslim lands, deeply religious men became sufis (mystics). They spent their time in prayer, or meditating on the words of the Qur'an.

Children in 16th-century Turkey (above) carrying the Qur'an through the streets to collect money for charity.

Holy words: (below) 'In the name of God, the merciful, the compassionate', written in Arabic in three different styles of calligraphy.

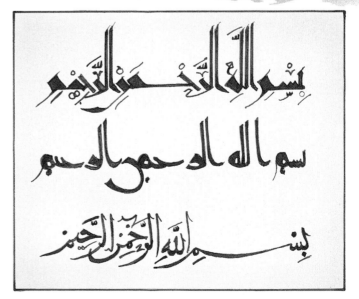

Muslim scribe (left) at his desk, from a 16th-century Turkish manuscript. He works seated on the floor, using a brush or reed pens and ink made of vinegar and soot. He has scissors, to cut the parchment he writes on, and a knife to scrape off any mistakes.

Decorative endpapers (far left) from a copy of the Qur'an. Muslims believed the Qur'an was the word of God, so copies of it were made as beautiful as possible.

Jewel-encrusted gold binding (left), made for a copy of the Qur'an read at Suleyman II's court. Muslims liked to give the Qur'an special bindings, because its words were so precious to them.

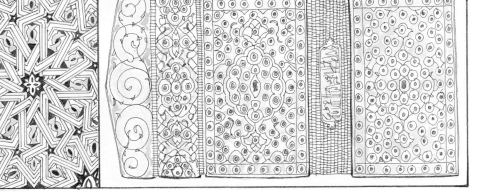

MEDICINE AND CHARITY

Giving to charity was an important religious duty for every Muslim who could afford it. Many individual men and women gave generously; local communities also collected charity tax. Traditionally, this was a small percentage (perhaps 5%) of a person's spare income.

Rulers like Suleyman, who were rich enough to pay for mosques, also gave money to maintain their new buildings. Suleyman's gift included farms, shops, inns along pilgrim routes and even whole villages. All this property was rented out and provided an income to pay for the upkeep of the mosque and the wages of people who worked there. It also paid for the primary school, the four medreses, and all the other mosque buildings serving the community.

The most important of these were a hospital, a rest-house for travelers, and a vast soup-kitchen, 105 feet long and 26 feet wide, which fed the medrese students and hundreds of poor citizens. There were also public baths, a sports ground, and the leading medical school in the Ottoman empire, where doctors were trained.

Muslim scholars were famous throughout the world, even in lands like Europe and China where most people followed different faiths. Muslim astronomers, geographers and doctors were especially skilled. Many Muslim mosques had fine libraries, full of books on a wide range of subjects.

A large mosque might have many different buildings attached, all serving the needs of the Muslim community. Money to build and maintain mosques came from gifts from wealthy Muslims.

This 16th-century manuscript picture (right) shows astronomers at the Ottoman royal observatory.

An astrolabe (below), used to measure the position of the stars, made around 850.

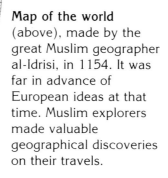

Map of the world (above), made by the great Muslim geographer al-Idrisi, in 1154. It was far in advance of European ideas at that time. Muslim explorers made valuable geographical discoveries on their travels.

Diagram of the human digestive system (right) drawn by a 17th-century Muslim doctor.

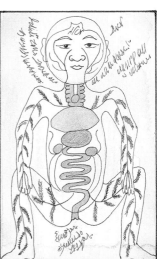

MOSQUES AROUND THE WORLD

In this book, we have seen how mosques developed from small, simple houses to magnificent public buildings in the centuries following the Prophet Muhammad's death in 632. We have also seen how mosques designed and built in one Muslim state – the Ottoman empire – made good use of local artistic traditions as well as the heritage of Christian buildings surviving from earlier centuries.

Mosque in Timbuktu, Mali (above), an important medieval city. It is built of clay bricks in West African style.

South-western Chinese mosque (right), built with steep, curving roofs, like traditional Chinese pagodas and temples.

The Mohammed Ali mosque (left), in Cairo, was built between 1824 and 1857. It is sometimes also known as the Alabaster Mosque.

The Selimiye mosque at Edirne, Turkey (right), built by Sinan between 1569-1575, for Sultan Selim II. Outside, it looks grand and important. Inside, it is light, elegant and spacious. Sinan declared it was his masterpiece.

Mosque in West Africa (above), thatched with bundles of grass.

Indonesian mosque (right), built of bamboo and palm-leaf thatch.

Local building styles also influenced mosque design in many other Muslim countries, from North Africa to the Far East. Architects employed craftsmen trained in traditional techniques. They used locally-available materials – palm thatch, mud bricks and bamboo poles. Inevitably, these affected mosque design; for example, where stone was scarce, massive walls and domed roofs could not be built. Like Sinan, these local architects used traditional patterns to decorate their mosques.

Mosque built in a mixture of styles, Kano, Nigeria (below). The walls are like traditional African buildings; the domes show Ottoman influence.

The mosque in Regent's Park, London (above), built 1977-1980. Today Muslim people live and worship in most parts of the world. Approximately one person in seven is a Muslim.

There was another, religious, reason why mosques were built in local styles. For many Muslims, practicing their faith was an essential part of their daily lives. Building a mosque that reflected local traditions was a sign of this.

The mosques designed for Ottoman sultans during the sixteenth century have been acclaimed as some of the world's greatest Islamic buildings. But thousands of equally beautiful mosques have been built since then in many Muslim lands.

King Hassan II of Morocco's mosque (left), in Casablanca, is built of pink marble. It is large enough to hold 100,000 worshippers.

GLOSSARY

Abstract pattern, a pattern based on simple shapes and lines, which does not portray any recognizable person, animal, plant or object.

AH, used to show years counted according to the Muslim calendar, which begins in AD 622, the year of the Hijra (see below).

Allah, the Arabic word for 'God', used by Muslims. Muslims believe that there is only one God, the creator of the world, and that he is merciful and compassionate. Throughout this book, the English word 'God' has been used to translate the Arabic word 'Allah'.

Alum, a white, powdery chemical. When mixed with dyes, it makes them color fabric permanently.

Apothecary, chemist.

Aquamanile, jug shaped like an animal. Mostly used for water.

Astronomy, the study of the stars and planets.

Bronze, a yellowish-brown metal, made of a mixture of copper and tin.

Buttress, a wall or block of brick or stone built up against another part of a building to support it.

Byzantine, belonging to Byzantium, the old (Greek) name for the city of Constantinople, which today is called Istanbul.

Caliph, the most powerful ruler in the Muslim world. He also had responsibilities to defend the Islamic faith.

Calligraphy, beautiful writing. Muslim scribes were world-famous for calligraphy.

Ceramic, made of pottery (baked clay).

Devout, devoted to religion.

Devshirme, the system of enslaving young men from Christian countries to be trained as Ottoman soldiers.

Dikka, a platform in a mosque where a Qari stood to repeat prayers or sermons to people sitting too far away from the Imam to hear them.

Diwan, a meeting of advisors at a ruler's court.

Dome, a type of roof, shaped like half a sphere; that is, like half a hollow ball.

Fasting, going without food and drink, and giving up other pleasures, to show obedience to God. Muslims fast during daylight hours in the month of Ramadan, the ninth month of the Islamic year.

Fix, (of dyeing) to make permanent.

Flagons, containers, often shaped like jugs, but with stoppers.

Floral, based on flowers.

Furnace, a stove, fueled by wood or coal.

Glazier, a craftworker who works with glass.

Grille, a decorative metal screen.

Hijra, the journey made by the Prophet Muhammad from Mecca to Medina in AD 622/1 AH to set up the first Muslim community.

Hospice, a place where people who are very ill are cared for.

Imam, prayer leader. A well-respected man chosen from among members of the Muslim community to lead communal prayers on Fridays, and to preach a sermon. Imams sometimes also acted as spokesman for local Muslim community groups. Imams were not priests. Unlike priests, they were not ordained (blessed and made holy at a special service). Any devout, learned man might be chosen for this role.

Incense, powdery or waxy substance burned to create clouds of sweet-smelling smoke.

Inscriptions, carved or painted writing, used as a form of decoration.

Islam, the faith preached by the Prophet Muhammad and taught by the Qur'an. The word 'Islam' means 'submission' or 'obedience' to God. Muslims try to live in a way the Qur'an tells them will be pleasing to God.

Islamic, belonging to Islam. 'Islamic' is used for things and ideas; 'Muslim' is used to describe people.

Iznik, a town in Turkey where a very skilled community of potters lived. The pottery they produced was known as 'Iznik style' and was heavily decorated.

Janissaries, a troop of soldiers in the Ottoman army. It was recruited from boys taken under the devshirme system. They were converted to Islam, and given a good training. Janissaries were highly respected; Sinan was one before he became an architect.

Kaaba, a holy building in the center of the city of Mecca, visited by Muslim pilgrims. Muslims believe that God was first worshipped there.

Kilim, a type of rug made in Turkey and Central Asia. Unlike a carpet, it does not have a velvety pile.

Kursi, a special bookrest, which held a copy of the Qur'an.

Mamelukes, the rulers of Egypt. Originally Turkish slaves, they became powerful and ended up running the country.

Medrese, a college, often attached to a mosque, where senior students went to continue their studies.

Mihrab, a niche in a mosque wall, showing the direction of the holy city of Mecca.

Minaret, a tall tower, part of a mosque, usually containing stairs and with a covered platform at the top. The place where muezzins stood to call Muslims to prayer.

Minbar, a raised platform in a mosque, reached by steps, from which Imams preached sermons.

Molten, melted.

Mosaic, picture or pattern created using many small pieces of glass, tile or stone.

Mosque, the building where Muslim people gather to say prayers. The word 'mosque' comes from the Arabic 'masjid' – a place where people bow down.

Muhammad, a man who lived in Arabia between AD c.570-632. After a series of revelations, he began to preach. He became leader of the first Muslim community (in Medina, in Arabia). He was (and is) honored throughout the Muslim world as the last and final prophet (messenger) sent by God to teach people how to live and worship.

Muslim, a follower of the faith of Islam. That is, someone who sincerely believes that 'There is no God but Allah [God], and Muhammad is the messenger of God.'

Niche, a hollowed out space in a wall.

Ottoman, the ruling family of Turkey and many neighboring lands, from the fifteenth to the early twentieth centuries.

Pagoda, a tower-shaped temple with several curving roofs built by people of the Buddhist faith. Found in China and India.

Pendentive, the stonework or brickwork between the base of a dome and the square building it rests on.

Persian, belonging to Persia (the former name for Iran).

Pier, a strong pillar or post.

Pile, the furry, velvety surface of carpets and other cloth.

Pilgrimage, a journey for religious reasons to a holy place.

Plaque, a flat panel, decorated with pictures, patterns or inscriptions, fixed onto a wall.

Prayer-rug, a rug used by most Muslims to cover the ground when they said their prayers five times a day. Often, prayer rugs were decorated with a minbar-shaped design in an elaborate border.

Prophet, someone who believes they have a message from God, which it is their duty to share with the world. Muslims believe that Abraham, Moses and Jesus, whose lives are described in the Bible and the Qur'an, were all prophets.

Qadi, scholar who had spent many years studying Islamic law (Shariya) and who acted as a judge in Islamic courts.

Qari, a man who loudly repeated the prayers and sermons spoken by an Imam so that all worshippers could hear them.

Qibla, the wall of a mosque that contains the mihrab. The qibla wall faces towards Mecca.

Qur'an, the holy book of Islam. Muslims believed that its words were revealed to the Prophet Muhammad in a series of visions from God. The Qur'an contains prayers, verses praising God, and instructions on how to live. Muslims believed that following the teachings of the Qur'an was the right way to live.

Rakat, a series of words and movements, used by Muslims when praying.

Reed pens, lengths of reed, trimmed to a point at one end by a knife.

Revelation, knowledge given to a person by God, sometimes in a vision or dream.

Scabbard, a close-fitting cover for a sword, often worn on a belt.

Sermon, a short talk on a religious topic, given by an Imam (and by religious leaders of many other faiths).

Shahada, Muslims' statement of what they believe: 'There is no God but Allah [God], and Muhammad is the messenger of God'.

Sharia, Islamic law. It was based on the Qur'an and on traditional sayings (hadith) of the Prophet Muhammad. It dealt with all areas of peoples' lives, not just religious matters.

Sufi, a Muslim mystic. Someone who spent long years praying, studying, meditating and (in some countries) dancing to try and find a way of feeling closer to God.

Sultan, king or emperor.

Tughra, a decorative way of signing the Ottoman sultan's name, used to show that royal documents were genuine.

Turban, a hat made of a long strip of cloth wound round the head, worn by men. Ottoman emperors decorated their turbans with beautiful jeweled pins.

Türbe, a small building, often circular or eight-sided and beautifully decorated with stone carvings or colored tiles, containing the tombs of important people. Most common in Turkey and Central Asia, but also found in other Muslim lands.

Vat, a very large container for liquids.

Wick, a short length of thread floating in a jar of oil. When set on fire, it gives out light.

Zakat, a tax collected in Muslim lands from wealthy people. The money was given to charity.

DATES IN THIS BOOK

In many Western countries, dates are calculated using a calendar that measures time from the birth of Jesus Christ, that is, from the year AD 1. 'AD' is short for 'Anno Domini', which means 'the year of the lord'. The years before Jesus's birth are labeled BC (Before Christ). This calendar was originally Christian, but has no religious meaning for many people today.

The Islamic calendar, used by Muslims worldwide, measures time differently, and still keeps its religious meaning. It starts in the year of the Hijra (migration), when the Prophet Muhammad left the Arabian city of Mecca to set up the first-ever community of Muslims in Medina. (You can read about Muhammad and his life on pages 6-7.) Muslims call this year 1 AH ('Anno Hegirae': 'the year of the Hijra'.) In the AD-BC calendar, it is AD 622.

There is another important difference between the Muslim and AD-BC calendars. AD-BC years are based on the sun, with 365 or 366 days; Islamic years are based on the moon, and contain 354 days. This makes it rather complicated to convert dates from one calendar to the other.

In this book, all the dates are given according to the AD-BC calendar. But here are the most important dates in the book, converted to AH:

AD 622/1AH	The Hijra
AD 632/10 AH	The Prophet Muhammad dies
AD 1453/857 AH	Ottomans capture Constantinople
AD 1491/896 AH	Architect Sinan Pasha born
AD 1494/899 AH	Suleyman the Magnificent born
AD 1520/926 AH	Suleyman the Magnificent becomes Sultan
AD 1557/965 AH	Suleymaniye Mosque completed
AD 1566/974 AH	Suleyman the Magnificent dies
AD 1588/997 AH	Architect Sinan Pasha dies

INDEX

Page numbers in bold refer to illustrations.

ST. JOHN THE BAPTIST ELEMENTARY
LIBRARY MEDIA CENTER